# Aural Piano Tuning
## A Practical Guide

### Rick Butler, RPT

ISBN number 1-59872-044-9

Copyright 2004 by Richard Butler
Revised 2005

Richard Butler is a Registered Piano Technician of
The Piano Technicians Guild

# ADDITIONAL BOOKS AND VIDEOS BY RICK BUTLER

## DVD's
Aural Piano Tuning

Voicing the Grand Piano

~

## AVAILABLE SOON

### Books
Action Geometry, Regulation and Voicing

Grand Dampers, Lyres and Trapwork

Rebuilding the Grand Piano
A step by step Procedure

www.rickbutler.org

# Dedication

This book – indeed, my career as a piano technician – would not have been possible without the continuing support and example of Wendell Eaton. His lifelong dedication to the highest standards in piano technology has helped inspire the success of many in our field. In my own case, he was there to teach me the basics when I first discovered the inside of a piano. His methodical approach, superb technical skills, and critical ear helped me tackle new challenges with humility, but also with confidence that there are no "exotic diseases" affecting pianos. To his many national honors and titles, I humbly add: Thank you, my cherished friend.

To the many other colleagues who have helped me refine or rethink a concept or procedure, my debt is great. Of long-standing support, particular thanks go to Orman Pratt, who taught me to appreciate the beautiful sound of a well-tuned piano; to Pat Stone, whose shop and mine were connected by a lifeline of shared technical discussions; and to Leo LaSota, my reality check for things musical and otherwise.

I also want to publicly recognize my sons, Ricky, John and David, for their time, effort, and understanding as they helped with the family business; my brothers Greg and Rodney, both of whom are professional piano technicians; and my wonderful wife, Patty, for her steadfast support in all facets of life's journey.

# Contents

Preface.................................................................. 2

Introduction........................................................... 4

Keyboard Nomenclature........................................ 5

A Dynamic Pattern for Tuning a Piano..................9

Hearing Beats & Controlling the Tuning Hammer.. 13

Tuning Octaves, Fourths and Fifths................... 27

Advanced Temperment...................................... 39

Tuning the Bass................................................. 59

Tuning the Treble............................................... 67

Tuning the Unisons............................................ 77

Appendix............................................................91

# Preface

I decided to write this book on aural piano tuning for several reasons. I have two sons who are following me in my profession. They work in my rebuilding shop, doing everything from minor repairs to major rebuilding. They're installing new soundboards, bridges, pinblocks and actions. One of the last steps in their training will be learning to tune. So, this book is primarily for them.

Another reason for this book is to serve my profession. With the electronic tuning devices being so popular, fewer tuners are tuning aurally. In order to become certified as a *"Registered Piano Technician"* in the Piano Technicians Guild, you must know how to tune aurally. You can not pass your certification examinations without knowing how to tune aurally.

Electronic tuning devices definitely have their place in this profession. I have one, and use it regularly. But I don't use it all the time. They're a wonderful teaching aid. They will teach you a lot about your own tuning. They will help you improve your skill. An electronic tuning device in the hands of an aural tuner is a wonderful tool.

I hope this book along with other instructional aids, will encourage everyone, and especially those "Associate" members of *The Piano Technicians Guild*, to take their certification examinations.

I wish you every success.

*Rick Butler*

# Introduction

Learning to tune pianos might be compared to learning how to ski. At first your teacher appears to be of little help. Explaining each individual step, your told to:

    Bend your knees.
    Look down the hill.
    Keep your weight on the downhill ski.
    Keep your back straight - but lean forward.

How can you think about all of that and still ski? You don't!

Here's the point: when you ski down the mountain you're not thinking about each individual step. You forget all the individual steps that, together, enable you to perform all of them with ease and grace.

However, in order to forget them as separate, individual steps, you must **first** learn them as **separate, individual** steps. Then you can put them together to become a graceful skier. Learning to tune pianos is similar. We will learn the steps individually and then put them together into one smooth motion.

This process takes time and effort. Set aside time every day to practice.

# Keyboard Nomenclature

I have decided to follow a "non-musical" standard for designating intervals we will be tuning. For our musical friends it will seem a bit awkward. The diagram on the next page illustrates the nomenclature we will follow. For the sake of simplicity, all the black notes on the piano keyboard will be referred to as sharps (#'s). This means for example, that A# below middle C up to F above middle C will be referred to as a "Fifth". Musically speaking, this is incorrect. Bb below middle C up to F above middle C is a "Fifth". However, Bb and A# are physically the same note on the modern piano keyboard. If as a musician, you find this somewhat annoying, I understand. I have a musical background and it takes some getting use too. It just doesn't seem right to refer to any interval by using a non-musical standard. But musicians can understand how non-musicians will find this system easy to grasp. If you're not a musician, it might seem confusing to refer to the same note on a keyboard by two different names. In any event, I hope this system will be easy for you to follow.

The intervals we will be using in this book will be defined and discussed later on.

# Naming Keys on the Standard Keyboard

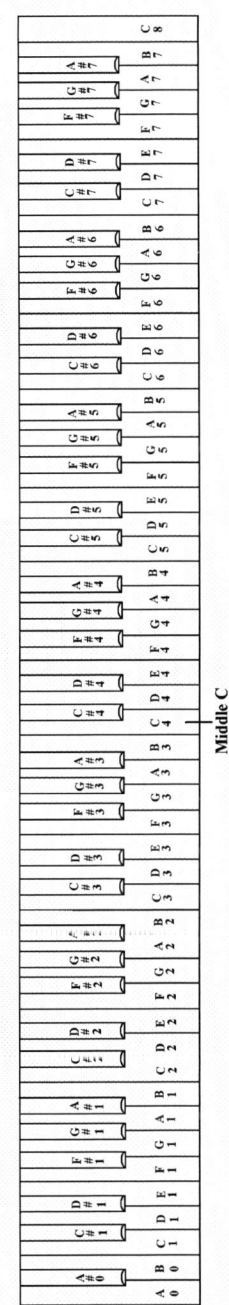

**This course will not use normal musical notation. All the black notes will be referred to as sharps.**

The first C on the keyboard is C1. The second key is C2, and so forth. The 3 notes below C1 are A0, A#0 and B0. The last C on the keyboard is C8.

# A Dynamic Pattern
## for
# Tuning a Piano

# Dynamic Tuning

This book presents a pattern of tuning that allows for the most efficient use of acoustical energy while achieving the greatest possible consonance. We want our completed tuning to accomplish the following objectives:

1. To make the fifths and octave-fifths as pure as possible, and at the same time, keep the octaves musically pleasing.
2. To make all the thirds, sixths, tenths and seventeenths beat progressively faster as you move chromatically up the keyboard, and slower as you move down the keyboard.

This pattern of tuning will allow for appropriate tests that can be applied rapidly, and will produce effective results. Important to this procedure is *strip mut-*

*ing the entire scale.* The center string of each trichord unison is tuned first. This allows for the outside strings of each unison to be tuned to the same reference note. Also, strip muting the entire scale will enable us to conveniently conduct tests to check our work as we progress through the tuning.

It must be noted that a piano must be in good tune in order for you to do a fine tuning. That means if a piano is off pitch, it will require a number of preliminary tunings to stabilize the instrument before such a fine tuning may be performed.

After strip muting the entire scale, we will use an A440 tuning fork to establish pitch on the piano. We will then set the notes between F3 and F4. From there we will tune the bass, then move up the treble to the last note, C8. From C8 we will tune the unisons down to the last note in the tenor. Finally we will tune the unisons in the bass.

I recommend that the piano you use to learn to

tune this dynamic pattern is in good condition. It should be at pitch. If it's not, have it tuned before you begin and why not observe the technician as he goes about the process. It should be a well-scaled instrument, which generally means that the piano is not too small, perhaps a 5'2" grand, or a 45" vertical piano. It should be a piano dedicated to your use. However, I understand that the ideal piano is not always possible, so use whatever piano is available.

# Hearing Beats
## and
# Controlling The Tuning Hammer

# Frequency

When you strike a string it moves back and forth. Frequency is the number of times, or cycles a string goes back and forth in a second. Cycles per second is abbreviated as **cps**.

## Pitch

Pitch is the word we use to describe the level of frequency. The higher the frequency the higher the pitch; the lower the frequency the lower the pitch.

The standard pitch is A440. That is A above middle C vibrates at 440 cycles per second. Many orchestra conductors ask that the piano be tuned to A442 or even higher.

## What are "Beats"?

Beats might be described as rhythmic pulses. They are perceived by our ears as a variation in loudness.

When two strings of a unison are tuned to exactly the same frequency, the two strings should sound as one single unwavering tone.

In order to aurally tune a piano, one must learn to recognize "beats".

Now, let's suppose that two strings are not at exactly the same frequency. One string is vibrating at 440 **cps**, the other is vibrating at 444 **cps**. The difference is four **cps**. Instead of a single unwavering tone, we now hear four beats per second in the tone.

It sounds like:
wah,wah,wah,wah
wah,wah,wah,wah
wah,wah,wah,wah

If one string is vibrating at 440 **cps,** and the other string is at 443 **cps**, we will hear three beats per second.

It sounds like:
wah,wah,wah
wah,wah,wah
wah,wah,wah

The beats are what we listen to in tuning the piano.

While we're talking about beats, the number of beats per second is abbreviated as **bps**. When tuning, we are usually comparing the beat rate of one interval against the beat rate of another interval. You only need to recognize or count one to twelve beats per second.

# False Beats

Sometimes a single string can have a beat in it. We call this a false beat. It does not have a single unwavering tone. This can occur in new as well as older pianos. It can occur in expensive as well as inexpensive pianos. You are more likely to find strings with false beats in the upper treble of the piano.

There are a number of reasons why a string can have a false beat:

1. The string or wire can be uneven in its diameter.
2. The string or wire may have been twisted when it was installed.
3. There could be a bend in the wire where there shouldn't be.
4. The string might not be seated properly on the bridge.
5. There may be a problem at the termination points of the string.

What do you do about false beats? Right now, nothing. I just want you to be aware that they occur. Sometimes, no matter what we do, we can't eliminate them. So, we recognize them and do the best we can to work around them.

# Partials and Harmonic Sequence

When a string is set in motion it vibrates as illustrated below.

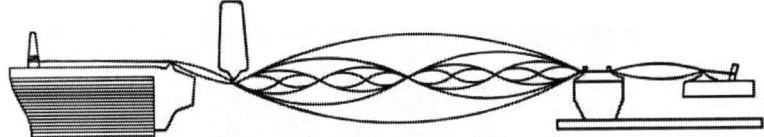

The string divides itself into **partials**. Notice the first partial is the fundamental.

| Example | Harmonic Sequence | Partial Number |
|---------|-------------------|----------------|
| A3 | Fundamental | 1 |
| A4 | Octave | 2 |
| E5 | Octave Fifth | 3 |
| A5 | Double Octave | 4 |
| C#6 | Double Octave Major Third | 5 |
| E6 | Double Octave Fifth | 6 |
| G6 | Double Octave minor Seventh | 7 |
| A6 | Triple Octave | 8 |

A **node** is a point on a vibrating string, that is free from vibratory motion. A node of a vibrating string has length and this length is not part of the speaking length of the string.

Example: A fourth partial has three nodes and two half nodes at each end. The fourth partial will have a speaking length of one-fourth of the first partial or fundamental.

## Learning to hear Beats

We stated that beats are rhythmic pulses, perceived as variations in loudness. Usually, each note or unison has three strings. So, take two rubber mutes and insert one between C4 (middle C) and B3, and one between C4 and C#4. This will block the left and right string of C4 and allow the center string to vibrate.

Now, play C4. You should hear a clean, steady and unwavering tone. Now, remove one of the mutes. Play the note again. Unless the note is in tune, you should hear a slow beat in the unison. You should hear a "wah,wah,wah,wah" in the unison.

As mentioned, there is the possibility that the unison is in tune, so you wouldn't hear any beats. Or, the difference in frequency is small, so the beat is very, very slow; that might make it difficult to hear the beats. If so, move the mutes around in the center section of the piano. You should hear some beats in some of the unisons. If not, don't worry. Read on because, if necessary, we will put some unisons out of tune.

Rubber Mute between Unisons

## What you need to do

1. Place the tuning hammer on the tuning pin of the right string of middle C.
2. Place the tuning hammer in the 1-2 o'clock position.
3. Play middle C and listen very carefully. Do you hear the beats?
4. If not, gently, push the tuning hammer in a counterclockwise direction. Please understand that you're only moving the tuning pin just a very little bit. Think of moving the pin in thousandths of and inch. You should now be comfortably assured that there are beats in this unison that you can hear.

## Exercise:

Practice listening to other notes by moving the mute to other unisons. Just stay within the middle range of the piano. Ask yourself how many beats there are per second. For example: Identify those unisons that sound clean and pure; those that have just a slow roll, less than 2 **bps**; and those that are beating at 2, 3, or 4 **bps**.

## Developing a tuning hammer technique

Think of the tuning hammer as that which is between the tuning pin and the beats that you hear. Controlling the beats means controlling the tuning pin. The tuning hammer allows you to do just that. This is not easy for two reasons:

1. The pin is held very tightly in the pinblock. Only the bottom half of the pin is in the pinblock. So, it's very easy to bend or flex the tuning pin. One must turn the pin in such a way that when you leave it, it will not move. Otherwise, the tuning will not be stable.
2. The string pulls the upper half of the pin towards the rear of the grand piano, and in a vertical towards the bottom of the piano

## Suggestions for Tuning Hammer Technique

Things to keep in mind about turning the tuning pin:

1. The resistance of the tuning pin to turn is very great and varies from piano to piano.
2. Once the resistance to turn is overcome, the tendency is for the pin to move too far.
3. Learn to turn the tuning pin in extremely small increments.

## When you want to move the tuning pin clockwise:

1. Grip the hammer with your fingers around the handle and your thumb extended to the left.
2. Pull primarily with your arm and shoulder.
3. At the same time, add to this pull a kind of jerk motion.*
4. Repeat this jerk motion with increasing intensity until the pin jumps, or stated another way, until you feel the entire pin move within the pin block.

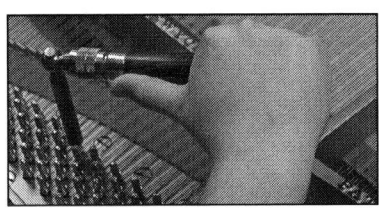

## When you want to move the pin counterclockwise:

1. Relax your grip and push the hammer with the palm or heel of your hand.
2. Push with your arm and shoulder.
3. At the same time add the jerk motion.
4. Repeat this jerk motion with increasing intensity.

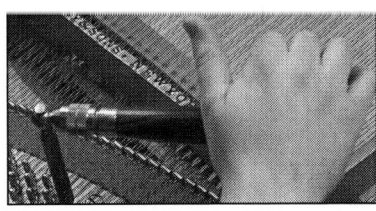

*This jerk motion allows you to overcome the resistance of the tuning pin without moving the pin too far. Always have in mind that the idea is to learn how to move the pin in extremely small increments.*

### Exercise #1

With your tuning hammer on an outside string in the 1-2 o'clock position, practice moving the pin and actually feeling the whole pin move. Listen to the beats as you do this, but remember the point of this exercise is to *feel the entire pin move within the pinblock*. In this exercise, we're not trying to tune the unison. We're only speeding up and slowing down the beat rate, not eliminating the beats.

### Exercise #2

Practice the following exercise to help you learn how to move the tuning pin in very small increments:

1. Play the key and make note of about how many beats there are per second.
2. Release the key.
3. Turn the tuning pin, without listening to the beats, to slow down the beats.
4. Play the key again and listen to the unison.
5. Repeat the above, but this time speed up the beats.

In this exercise I have asked you to separate listening to the unison and manipulating the pin. However, as I have already mentioned, as you gain experience you will combine all of these steps into one seamless procedure.

## How to determine which direction to turn the tuning pin to make the unison beatless: clockwise or counterclockwise.

1. Place the tuning hammer on the tuning pin in the one to two o'clock position.
2. Play the key and listen to the beats. *As the volume of the note fades, the beats will fade. Just play the note again. Continue listening while you do step three.*
3. Gently push or apply pressure on the tuning hammer. (counterclockwise) *This slight pressure or push of the hammer is not intended to turn the pin in the pin block. It is a slight momentary twisting or flexing of the pin.*
4. As you push or apply pressure, do the beats increase or decrease? *If the beats increase as you twist the pin counterclockwise, you know that the tuning pin needs to be turned clockwise to eliminate the beats.*
5. Relax or untwist the pin. (leave in the neutral position)
6. Play the key and slightly pull on the tuning hammer. (clockwise)
7. Listen to the beat rate.
8. Determine if the beat rate increases or decreases with this pull. *If the beats increase as you twist the pin clockwise, you then know that the tuning pin needs to be turned counterclockwise.*
9. Relax or untwist the pin. (leave in the neutral position)

You have now determined whether you need to turn the tuning pin clockwise or counterclockwise to eliminate the beats.

## Alternative Method to determine which direction to turn the tuning pin

Another way to determine if the note you want to tune is sharp or flat is to use an interval check. For example, drop down a major third (four notes below) and mute that unison so as to hear only one string. Now listen to each string of the unison in question using the third below as a reference note. The speed of the individual beat rates will tell you which direction to tune the string. Only use this test between C3 and F4. Later, you may choose to use other intervals to test the unisons, like Major Sixths, or Major Tenths. Your choice will depend on what area of the piano your are tuning.

---

### Exercise in Unison Tuning

Tune the unisons in the middle section of the piano. In this exercise, you will tune the outside strings to the center string. Eliminate the beats. Begin in the lower tenor section, and move chromatically up the scale. That will mean you will block the left string with the rubber mute, and tune the right string to the center. Then, remove the mute and block the right string you just tuned (and the left string of the next unison) and tune the left string. Proceed up the scale to the end of the middle section.

## Test Blow

When one strikes the key firmly, it is traditionally called a test blow. The purpose of this firm strike of the key is to equalize the tension along the entire length of the string. It has been said that this contributes to a stable tuning. Use this technique after the note has been tuned. Strike the key using the third and fourth fingers producing a moderately loud tone. Immediately strike the key again, this time producing a soft tone. Listen to the beats using this soft tone. Did the tuning change? If so, re-tune and apply another test blow.

Another effective style of test blow is to strike a cluster of keys around the note your tuning with the palm or fist of your hand. This method does not require you to strike the keys with such a strong blow.

Whether one is using the traditional test blow, or striking a cluster of keys with your palm or fist, remember; your hand is not a hammer. Avoid damaging your hand with strong repetitious blows to the keys.

Please note that a test blow may not always be necessary when fine tuning a piano. When the piano is already stable and in very good tune, feeling each tuning pin is perhaps the most important test.

# Review

Before you leave this section, you want to feel fairly comfortable tuning a unison. That will mean two things. You're hearing the beats, and feeling the tuning pin move inside the pinblock.

The quality of the tools you use is important. Invest in a professional tuning hammer with all of its accessories. You will be amazed at the difference between a hammer with a tip that fits the pin properly and one that doesn't. The length of the tuning lever makes a difference too. I carry two levers in my bag. One is the traditional length; the other is shorter.

Don't rush through this section. Exercise two on page 19 is extremely important. Really learn to move the tuning pin in very small increments. This is important in learning how to tune. Knowing what to do is the easy part. Executing it is another.

The chart on page 15 on partials is worth thinking about. Intervals have co-incidental partials. What are the co-incidental partials of an octave? What are the co-incidental partials of a Fifth or Fourth? When you grasp this, you will understand what beats you are hearing. However, don't get carried away with this, especially at this point.

One more time: **Concentrate on your tuning hammer control.** It's the key to progress!

# Tuning Octaves Fourths and Fifths

# Intervals

You've learned that unisons should be beatless intervals. Let's list the other intervals that we will use to tune the piano. These intervals are not beatless.

**Octaves** - just wide of beatless *Spans 13 notes (including the two notes being depresse*d)
**Fourths** - just wide of beatless - *Spans 6 notes*
**Fifths** - just narrow of beatless - *Spans 8 notes*
**Major Thirds** - wide of beatless - *Spans 5 notes*
**Minor Thirds** - narrow of beatless - *Spans 4 notes*
**Major Sixths** - wide of beatless - *Spans 10 notes*
**Tenths** - wide of beatless - *Spans 17 notes*
**Seventeenths** - wide of beatless - *Spans 29 notes*

There are some other intervals that we will use to tune with as well. For example the **Octave/Fifth**, which is an octave and a Fifth. Another, is a **double octave**, and still another is a **double octave plus a seventh**.

How wide is wide and how narrow is narrow? The piano will actually tell you the answer to that question, and it will vary from piano to piano. Later, we'll discuss how intervals like thirds, sixths, and tenths will have certain beat rates. By comparing these intervals to each other, you will be able to determine how wide or narrow the interval should be, or stated another way; by comparing these intervals, you can determine how fast or slow the beat rates should be. It is by comparing the beat rates of various intervals that we actually tune a piano. If this sounds a bit confusing, don't worry, you'll understand a little later on when we further explain the tuning process.

# Aural Interval Recognition

There are a minimum of three intervals that we should be able to aurally recognize. The Octave, Fifth and Fourth. How can you learn to recognize these intervals? One way is by association with popular melodies. In the examples below, the first pitch change of the melody represents the interval you would need to learn. You don't have to learn to sing them, but you should learn to hear them.

There are times when a piano is badly out of tune. One can only use beats to tune a note if it is not too far out of tune. If it is, tuning an interval using a melody will enable you to easily come close enough to the right pitch, and then switch to listening to the beats. This approach is also useful when chipping a piano. Chipping is a term that is used to describe the process of putting tension on the strings for the very first time.

## Melodies for the Fifth

*Twinkle Twinkle Little Star / My Favorite Things*
*People Will Say We're In Love / Stranger In Paradise*

## Melodies for the Fourth

*Here Comes The Bride*
*Match Maker (from Fiddler on the Roof) / Taps*

## Melodies for the Octave

*Over The Rainbow / The Rain in Spain / Camelot*

## Tuning the Octave

An octave spans 13 notes and should be just wide of beatless. However, it should be perceived as beatless. Therefore, the beat would be more like a wave, rather than a beat, and a slow wave at that. Use the "**M3/M10**" test to confirm the octaves in the middle and lower sections of the piano. It is not the only test we will use to confirm an octave. We will introduce a few others later.

---

### What you need to learn.

The "**Major Third / Major Tenth**" test. **M3/M10**

Compare the beat rate of the M3 to the M10.
The M3 should be slower than the M10.

Example: A3 / A4 octave;   F3 to A3 should be slower than F3 to A4

The reference note is always a major third below the lower note of the octave being checked.

If F3/A4 is faster than F3/A3 the octave is wide.
If F3/A4 is slower than F3/A3 the octave is narrow.
If F3/A4 is the same as F3/A3 the octave is perfect.

## Exercise:

Insert a felt muting strip usually called "the temperment strip" between <u>all</u> of the unisons in the middle section of the piano. This will allow the center string of each unison to vibrate, while the outside strings are muted.

Beginning with the first steel string unison in the tenor, tune the octaves up to the last unison in the tenor before the tenor/treble break. That is, tune the upper note to the lower note. If the first note in the tenor is F2, then put your tuning hammer on F3. Tune F3 using F2. Then move the tuning hammer to F#3. Now tune F#3 using F#2. Continue up the scale until you reach the break. Check each octave as you go with the M3/M10 test. Make M10 faster than the M3, but not so fast that the octave has an unacceptable beat.

Insert the felt strip between the unisons.

## Tuning Fourths and Fifths

**Fifths** are just a bit narrow of perfect, about ½ beat a second (1 beat in 2 seconds).

**Fourths** are just a bit wide of perfect, about ¾ beat a second (3 beats in 4 seconds).

========================================

Example of tuning a Fifth:
1. Tune F3 using C4 beatless.
2. Re-tune F3 by slightly raising the pitch to 1 beat in 2 seconds.

> **What you need to learn.**
> Tune "Fifths" narrow of perfect.
> Tune "Fourths" wide of perfect.

Let's turn this example around.
1. Tune C4 using F3 beatless.
2. Retune C4 by slightly lowering the pitch to 1 beat in 2 seconds.

**The idea is to make the interval of a "Fifth" narrow of beatless.**

========================================

Example of tuning a Fourth:
1. Tune G3 using C4 beatless.
2. Re-tune G3 by slightly lowering the pitch to 3 beats in 4 seconds.

Let's turn this example around.
1. Tune C4 using G3 beatless.
2. Re-tune C4 by slightly raising the pitch to 3 beats in 4 seconds.

**The idea is to make the interval of a "Fourth" wide of beatless.**

## Exercise:
(For the middle section of the piano.)

Step 1
- Tune F4 using F3. Check this octave with the M3/M10 test.
- Tune C4 using F3 (Fifth).
Check C4 to F4 (Fourth).

Step 2
- Tune F#4 using F#3. Check this octave with the M3/M10 test.
- Tune C#4 using F#4 (Fourth).
- Check C#4 to F#3 (Fifth).

Step 3
- Proceed up the keyboard as outlined in steps 1 and 2.

# Setting the Pitch

There are a number of different ways to set the pitch of a piano. Since this course is about aural tuning, we will use a tuning fork. Our choice will be a A440 tuning fork. A440 corresponds with A4 on the piano

### Procedure for setting pitch.

1. Mute F2 and A4 so that only one string of each unison is free to vibrate.
2. Hold the tail of the fork with your right hand and strike it against your knee or elbow.
3. Place the fork on the bridge or another wood surface to amplify the sound.
4. Play F2 and listen to the beat rate between F2 and the tuning fork.*
5. Now play F2 and A4. Is the beat rate the same as F2 to the A440 fork?
6. Tune A4 using F2 to the same beat rate as F2 to the tuning fork.
7. Check: Strike the fork, hold it close to your ear, and play A4. It should be beatless.
8. Tune the unison of A4.
9. Repeat step 7. If A4 has moved, repeat the whole procedure.

*If the beat rate is too fast or too slow, adjust the beat pitch of F2 so that the beat rate between F2 and the fork is about 7 beats per second (bps).*

# Equal Temperment
## Fourths and Fifths

The system used today to tune a piano is based upon the "Equal Temperment", which theoretically divides the octave into 12 evenly spaced semi-tones.

With the middle section of the piano strip muted, follow this procedure as an exercise. Remember the Fifth is narrow and the Fourth is wide. This is the first of two procedures for setting the temperment that this book presents.

## Fourth and Fifth Temperment

1. Set A4 to pitch
2. Tune A3 using A4
3. Check A3/A4 octave using the M3/M10 test.
4. Tune E4 using A3 (Fifth)
5. Tune D4 using A3 (Fourth)
6. Tune G3 using D4 (Fifth)
7. Tune C4 using G3 (Fourth)
8. Tune F3 using C4 (Fifth)
9. Tune F4 using F3 Octave
10. Check F3/F4 octave using M3/M10 test.
11. Tune A#3 using F4 (Fifth)
12. Tune D#4 using A#3 (Fourth)
13. Tune G#3 using D#4 (Fifth)
14. Tune C#4 using G#3 (Fourth)
15. Tune F#3 using C#4 (Fifth)
16. Tune B3 using F#3 (Fourth)
17. Check B3 to E4 (Fourth)

## What if step 17 does not check out?

Go through the temperment sequence again, but this time go backwards.  Start at step 17, and end with step 1.

## What do you need to do next?

With the piano at pitch and a workable temperment on the piano:

1. Tune the octaves up to the tenor/treble break.
2. Tune down to the tenor/bass break.
3. Use the M3/M10 test to check all octaves.
4. Remove the temperment strip and tune all unisons

## A suggested procedure for pianos that are badly out of tune.

When a piano is badly out of tune or off pitch, it needs to be raised in pitch.  A piano which needs to be raised in pitch will require more than one tuning.  There are many approaches to raising pitch, or pre-tuning a piano.  One approach is presented on page 81.  If your goal is to tune the piano to A440, you would want to begin at a higher pitch than A440, perhaps A442, or A444.  The added tension on the piano will cause the pitch to drop somewhat.  You want it to settle on your pre-determined pitch.  Occasionally, you will need two or more tunings to stabilize the instrument before it can be finely tuned.

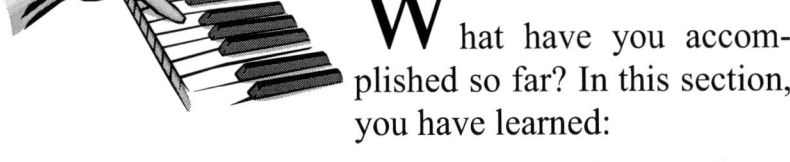

# Review

What have you accomplished so far? In this section, you have learned:

- Which intervals we will be using and how to figure them out on the keyboard.
- To tune the basic intervals of the Octave, Fourth, and Fifth.
- The "**Major Third / Major Tenth**" test. <u>**M3/M10.**</u>
- To set the pitch on the piano.
- And establish a temperment on the piano.

So, do you understand what you've accomplished? You probably can carry everything forward and at least rough tune the entire piano! That's pretty important. Why? Many pianos you come across in the field are not on pitch. Often, they are anywhere from 1/8 to 1/2 step off pitch. Sometimes more. You can't fine tune a piano that far out of tune. So, you need to get the piano close to pitch. <u>Now you can</u>. Understand there is a difference between raising pitch and fine tuning. Raising pitch is simply rough tuning a piano. Sometimes you may have to tune the piano twice, or even three times to have it stable at A440. Then you can fine tune the instrument.

The next sections will present additional interval tests to check your work up and down the keyboard. But remember:

**<u>Concentrate on your Tuning Hammer Control.</u>**

# Advanced Temperment

# Advanced Temperment

The "Advanced Temperment" will be presented in four parts. Part I will probably be the most challenging. Part II will tell you if you have part I correct. If it's not correct, you will have an idea of what adjustments you will need to make in order to make the first two parts work together. Once you have completed these two parts, the next two steps will be relatively easy to achieve.

### The advanced temperment (F3 to F4) will achieve the following:

1. As you move chromatically up the keyboard all Major thirds will progressively beat faster.
2. As you move chromatically down the keyboard all Major thirds will progressively beat slower.
3. As you move chromatically up the keyboard all Major sixths will progressively beat faster.
4. As you move chromatically down the keyboard all Major sixths will progressively beat slower.
5. The Fifths will have a very clean sound.
6. The Fourths will have a slow beat.

# Advanced Temperment Part I

The **foundation** of our equal temperment begins with a series of thirds. They are as follows:

### F3/A3 - A3/C#4 - C#4/F4

F3/A3 will beat about 7 bps
A3/C#4 will beat about 9bps
C#4/F4 will beat about 11bps

Do you actually count 7, 9, and 11 beats per second? You might count them when you first begin to tune. But eventually, you'll learn to recognize what 7 bps sounds like. You'll learn to recognize the speed of the other two intervals as well.

Although it might seem difficult to establish the speed of these thirds, it's not as difficult as it might seem. Why? Because these thirds must fit between the F3 and F4 octave. We have already learned to tune an octave and confirm it with the M3/M10 test. So, it's just a matter of balancing the speed of these thirds within the octave. The A3/C#4 third is faster than the F3/A3 third as the C#4/F4 third is faster than the A3/C#4 third.

*Sometimes, you will find, particularly on smaller pianos, that you will need to vary the ratio of these thirds. The F3/A3 will usually work at about 7 bps. But, the A3/C#4 third might need to be a little faster, and the C#4/F4 third even faster yet. That would mean the octave would have to be expanded a little bit more. How will you know when you will need to make such adjustments? You will know when you're working on Part II of the Advanced Temperment. But for now, make this series of thirds evenly spaced. We'll discuss such variations in Part II.*

**Learn part I of the "Advanced Temperment"**

1. **Tune** A4 using the tuning fork
2. **Tune** A3 using A4
3. Confirm the A3/A4 octave using the M3/M10 test
4. **Tune** F3 using A3 to 7bps
5. **Tune** C#4 using A3 to 9bps
6. **Tune** F4 using C#3 to 11bps
7. Confirm the octave F3/F4, using the M3/M10 test

## Ask yourself...

Do I have this series of thirds,
*F3/A3 - A3/C#4 - C#4/F4*
**evenly spaced** between the octave F3/F4?

The F3/A3 - A3/C#4 ratio is 4/5
The A3/C#4 - C#4/F4 ratio is also 4/5

Is the speed of the beats about 7 - 9 - 11bps.

Does the F3/F4 octave check with the M3/M10 test?

### Helpful Hint:
4 **bps** can be counted as: Mississippi (4 syllables)
5 **bps** can be counted as: Ethiopia (5 syllables)

### What if the M3/M10 test is incorrect?
Do you need to raise or lower F3?
Do you need to lower or raise F4?

Go back and listen to the series of thirds again. Which third could be made slower or faster to make the **M3** **M10** test work?

Just remember three things:
- You don't want to change A3
- You must keep the 3 thirds evenly spaced.
- Make the M10 just faster than the M3, and still have a clean sounding octave.

## Advanced Temperment Part II

We will now add two more notes to our temperment sequence: F#3 and A#3, which together, make a major third. We will be using notes that have been tuned in Part I to tune these two notes.

As was mentioned earlier, part II will tell us if part I was tuned correctly. How? A#3 will be tuned using F4; a fifth. Then, F#3 will be tuned using C#4; a fifth. We have already learned to tune a fifth. Now, we will confirm these fifth intervals using the "Fifth Check", which is explained on the next page. Now, these two notes, F#3 and A#3, form a Major third. This third must be faster than the Major third below it. If we can't make an adjustment in either F#3 or A#3 to make this third faster than F3/A3, and still maintain the check for the Fifths, then we must go back and adjust the intervals in Part I.

So, before actually tuning the notes in Part II of the "Advanced Temperment", we need to learn the check for the "Fifth". Remember the "Fifth" is just narrow of beatless, and spans 8 notes. Although, we would like for the fifth to be perfect, that is not possible in the equal temperment. But, let's make the fifth as close to perfect as the piano will allow. Our checks will tell us how close to perfect we can make them.

## Learn the check for the Fifth.

The "**Major Sixth / Major Tenth**" test. **M6/M10**

This test compares the beat rate of the M6 to the M10. The M6 should beat faster than the M10.

The reference note on this test is always a major sixth below the lower note of the Fifth being checked, and a major 10 below the upper note.

*This reference note should be adjusted so that the speed of the beats is not to fast or slow to be of little value in making an accurate comparison.*

Example: F3 to C4 (Fifth)
G#2 will be the reference note in this example
G#2 to F3 (M6) should beat faster than G#2 to C4 (M10)

If G#2 to F3 is faster than G#2 to C4 the Fifth is narrow.
If G#2 to F3 is slower than G#2 to C4 the Fifth is wide.
If G#2 to F3 is the same as G#2 to C4 the Fifth is perfect.

## How much faster should the M6 be over the M10?

It will vary. For example, the test for the octave uses the M3/M10 test. In this test, the M10 is usually just a little faster than the M3. There's a bit more of difference in the speed between the M6 and the M10, in the Fifth test, than there is between the M3 and the M10 in the Octave test. But how much? Again it will vary with each piano.

We talked about how we might need to make a certain third beat a little faster than the one below it. Or, it might be beating a little too fast compared to the third below it. Therefore, you will need to adjust one or both of the notes in that particular third to make it fit with the third below or perhaps the third above it. How will this adjustment effect the checks that you used to confirm the Fifths related to each note in this third? Will the M6 still beat faster than the M10? Usually, you will see that there is some room for a little movement, and still have the M6 beat faster than the M10.

## Learn part II of the "Advanced Temperment"

8. **Tune** A#3 using F4 (Fifth)

9. *Check* the Fifth: use the **M6/M10** check *C#3 to A#3 (M6) should be faster than C#3 to F4 (M10).*

10. **Tune** F#3 using C#4

11. *Check* the Fifth: use the **M6/M10** check A2 to F#3 should beat faster than A2 to C#4

12. Now compare the Third F#3/A#3 to F3/A3 F#3/A#3 should be a bit faster than F3/A3

13. Use the above Fifth checks to determine how to adjust the speed of this Third.

A requirement of the "Advanced Temperment" is that the thirds beat faster as you move up the keyboard and slower as you move down the keyboard. Therefore, the speed of the thirds becomes a check in itself.

Make any adjustments to the third F#3/A#3 to make it a little faster than F3/A3, and still keep the checks for the Fifths, F#3/C#3 and A#3/F4 correct. When checking the Fifth, it's not necessarily important how much faster the M6 is above the M10, just that it is faster. Remember, the scale of the piano will determine what the beat rates will be. Usually, the larger pianos will have closer beat rates.

When you're wanting to make a change in the F#3/A#3 Third, listen to the Fifth checks to help you decide which note to change that will still maintain the requirements of the Fifth check, and, at the same time make the F#3/A#3 Third faster than the F3/A3 Third.

Suppose that you cannot make the F#3/A#3 third a little faster than the F3/A3 third, and still keep the fifths A#3/F4 and F#3/C#4 correct. Then we need to make adjustments to the first series of third we tuned in part I. What adjustments do we need to make? Here's what I would suggest:

1. Leave A3 where it is. Don't change it.
2. Leave F3 where it is. Don't change it.
3. Tune C#4 a little sharper. Make the A3/C#4 third faster.
4. Now the third C#4/F4 is beating slowly. Tune F4 so that the third C#4/F4 is beating faster than it was originally.
5. Now listen to the F3/F4 octave. Is the octave still acceptable? Use the **M3/M10** test to gauge how wide this octave really is.

We're trying to expand the F3/F4 octave. But there is a limit to what we will be able to do. If, after making the above adjustments you still can't make everything fit, try this:

1. Tune F3 a little sharp so as to slow the F3/A3 third down a little bit.
2. Tune C#4 to make the A3/C#4 third faster.
3. Tune F4 to make the C#4/F4 third faster.

Now you should be able to go back and make adjustments to F#3 and A#3 to make the F#3/A#3 third beat a little faster than the F3/A3 third, and still keep the fifths F#3/C#4 and A#3/F4 correct.

# Advanced Temperment Part III

We now add G#3 and D#4 to the temperment procedure. We will also begin to compare the speed of one sixth to another sixth, and the speed of a sixth to a third.

Preliminary to learning Part III, we need to learn how to confirm the tuning of our Fourths. Remember the Fourth spans 6 notes and beats wide of beatless. The Fourth should have a definite "roll" in it, three beats in four seconds. The Fourth is really an inversion of the Fifth. F up to C is a Fifth. C up to F is a Fourth. In the check for the Fifth, the smaller interval (M6) beats faster than the larger interval (M10). In the check for the Fourth, it's just the opposite. The smaller interval (M3) beats slower than the larger interval (M6).

We have already noted that the thirds beat progressively faster as you go up the keyboard and slower as you go down the keyboard. The same is true of the Sixths. They beat faster as you go up the keyboard and slower as you go down the keyboard\. You can now begin to picture in your mind that there is a relationship between the beat rates of sixths compared to the thirds.

# Learn the check for the Fourth.

The "**Major Third / Major Sixth**" test.  **M3/M6**

Compare the beat rate of the M3 to the M6.
The M3 should beat slower than the M6.

The reference note on this test is always a major third below the lower note of the Fourth being checked, and a major sixth below the upper note.

*This reference note should be adjusted so that the speed of the beats is not too fast or slow to be used to make an accurate comparison.*

Example: G#3 to C#3 (Fourth)
The reference note in this example is E3
E3 to G#3(M3) should beat slower than E3 to C#4 (M6)

## How much slower should the M3 be over the M6?

Again, it will vary just a little. The octave test compares the beat rate of the M3 to the M10. The M10 beats just a little faster than the M3. The Fifth test compares the M6 to the M10. The difference between these beat rates is usually a little more than the beat rates for the octave. The difference between beat rates in the Fourths test is usually a bit more than they are for the tests for the Fifths. So, how do you settle on the correct speed for the different beat rates? When you can make everything fit, you'll have it. When the Octave, Fifths and Fourths test all work together, that will be the correct speed. You're not likely to hit it correctly the first time around. Sometimes to make the fifths fit, you may have to go back and widen the temperment octave a little bit. If the fourths are too fast, you might have to go back and make the fifths a little more narrow. It's a balancing act.

Another useful tool is the sixths. As the beat rates of the thirds speed up and slow down as you play them chromatically up and down the keyboard, so do the sixths. You can also compare the beat rates of thirds to sixths. By listening to the outside sixths and inside thirds chromatically up and down the temperment octave, and even beyond, you will be able to hear where some adjustments will be needed. Even very experienced tuners will need to make some adjustments here or there.

---

### **Outside Major Sixth / Inside Major Third Check**

The **Outside Major Sixth / Inside Major Third** Check (<u>OM6/IM3</u>)

The outside sixth should be equal to the inside third. However, *please note that there will be occasions when you will find that the outside sixth will not quite match the inside third. This will often occur on those pianos where you had to expand the F3/F4 octave in part II.*

Example: F3/D4 (Outside M6) equals G3/B3 (Inside M3) <u>OM6/IM3</u>

---

**Outside Sixths / Inside Thirds** within the temperment.

F3/D4 = G3/B3
F#3/D#4 = G#3/C4
G3/E4 = A3/C#4
G#3/F4 = A#3/D4

This pattern can be expanded beyond the temperment!

**Learn part III of the "Advanced Temperment"**

14. **Tune** D#4 using A#3 (Fourth)
15. Use the M3/M6 test to check the Fourth. The reference note is F#3. F#3/A#3 is slower than F#3/D#4.
16. **Tune** G#3 using C#4 (Fourth)
17. Use the M3/M6 test to check the Fourth. The reference note is E3. E3/G#3 is slower than E3/G#3.
18. Check the Fifth G#3/D#4 (M6/M10 test) The reference note is B2. B2/G#3 (M6) is faster than B2/D#4.
19. Listen to the Sixth, G#3/F4 (M6). G#3/F4 should be a bit faster than A3/C#4 (M3).

What if you can't make the Fifth, G#3/D#4 correct and still make the Sixth G#3/F4 beat just a little faster than the Third A3/C#4? You probably need to make some adjustment in the series of thirds you made in Part I of the "Advanced Temperment". Try adjusting F4 to make the Sixth G#3/F4 beat a little faster than A3/C#4. Now make whatever adjustments to C#4 and F3 to balance the series of Thirds F3/A3-A3/C#4-C#4/F4.

Another option is to re-check the intervals in Part II of the "Advanced Temperment" to make sure there aren't any changes that would make things work out in Part III.

# Advanced Temperment Part IV
## Completing the temperment

We will now add C4, E4, D4, G3 and B3 to our sequence which will complete the temperment. You should find that these notes will fall into place rather easily. There aren't any new tests to learn either. You have all the tools you need to finish this octave.

When you are finished, you should have been able to accomplish the following:

1. As you move chromatically up the temperment the Major thirds should progressively beat faster.

2. As you move chromatically down the temperment the Major thirds should progressively beat slower.

3. As you move chromatically up the temperment the Major sixths should progressively beat faster.

4. As you move chromatically down the temperment the Major sixths should progressively beat slower.

5. The Fifths should have a clean sound.

6. The Fourths should have a slow beat or roll.

7. A consistent relationship between the Outside Sixths and Inside Thirds. Usually they will be equal.

8. The F3/F4 octave will be wide but very acceptable.

**Learn part IV of the "Advanced Temperment":**

20. **Tune** C4 using F3
21. *Check* the Fifth F3/C4
    (reference note is G#2)

22. **Tune** E4 using A3 (Fifth)
23. *Check* the Fifth A3/E4
    (reference note is C3)
24. *Check*: C4/E4 is slower than C#4/F4
    (progressive thirds)

25. **Tune** D4 using A3 (Fourth)
26. *Check* the Fourth (reference note is F3)
27. *Check*: A#3/D4 (M3) is faster than A3/C#4

28. **Tune**: G3 using C4 (Fourth)
29. *Check* the Fifth G/D
30. *Check* the Fourth (reference note is D#3)
31. *Check*: G3/E4 equals A3/C#4
    (outside sixth/inside third)
32. *Check*: D#3/G3 (M3)
    slower than D#3/C4 (M6)

33. **Tune** B3 using E3 (Fourth)
34. *Check*: F#3/B3 (Fourth)
35. *Check*: F3/D4 equals G3/B3

# Review

That was a lot to learn. It will take a while to digest all of it. So, what were you able to accomplish in this section?

- You learned what the beats in the temperment octave should sound like.
- You learned how to set the first series of thirds, which is *very* important.
- The "**Major Sixth / Major Tenth**" test (**M6/M10**).
- The "**Major Third / Major Sixth**" test. (**M3/M6**).
- The "**Outside Major Sixth/ Inside Major Third**" check (**OM6/IM3**)

Add to that the "**Major Third / Major Tenth**" test, (**M3/M10**) that you learned earlier, and you now have the tools to fine tune the middle of the piano. I know I keep reminding you that it's fairly easy to learn what to do, and another thing to execute it. So, be patient and practice every day. Concentrate on hammer control by moving the tuning pin in very small increments.

This temperment favors the Fifth over the

Fourth. Therefore, the Fourth will beat faster than the Fifth. However, you could tune the temperment so that the Fourths and Fifths beat about the same. Never though, allow the Fourth to beat slower than the Fifth. As you gain experience, you will be able to make this easily make this adjustment. All of the interval checks that have been presented will still apply. Please don't let these comments confuse you. I'm just letting you know ahead of time that you're not locked into a certain temperment. You may prefer the Fifths to beat about the same as the Fourths, but you may not.

Now, we're going to move to the bass section. The interval tests we use to tune the bass and the treble sections are based upon the intervals that are already set within the temperment. Therefore, if they're not correct, the interval tests for the bass and treble will not work out.

# Tuning
## the
# Bass

## Tuning E3 down to C2

The pattern for tuning this section will be as follows:

1. Tune the Octave
2. Listen to the Fifth
3. Listen to the Fourth
4. Listen to the Major Third
5. Listen to the minor Third
6. Compare the minor Third to the Major Sixth

Example: Tuning E3

1. Tune E3 using E4
2. Listen to E3/B3 (Fifth)
3. Listen to E3/A3 (Fourth)
4. Listen to E3/G#3 (Major 3rd)
5. Listen to E3/G3 (minor 3rd)
6. Listen to E3/G3
7. Listen to G3/E4

## What do you need to do?

Tune E3 down to C2 using the above instructions.

## What are you listening for?

- The Octave should be clean.

- The Fifth should be almost clean.

- The Fourth should have a slow beat

- The Major Third (step-4), should be slower than the Minor Third (step-5)

On pianos with a nice scale:

- The Minor Third (step-6) should be equal to the Major Sixth (step-7). However you will find that this check will not work on all pianos.

- Some pianos will only allow you to use steps 1-3 on this pattern.

# Tuning B1 down to C1

The pattern for tuning this section will be as follows:

1. Tune the Octave
2. Listen to the Fifth
3. Listen to the Fourth

Example: Tuning B2

1. Tune B2 using B3
2. Listen to B2/F#3 (Fifth)
3. Listen to B2/E3 (Fourth)

> **What do you need to do?**
>
> Tune E2 down to C1 using the above instructions.

## What are you listening for?

The Octave should be clean.
The Fifth should be almost clean.
The Fourth should have a slow beat

## Checking Bass Octaves

Bass Octaves can be checked by listening to the beats of the descending
**Octave-minor seventh**

Play C2/A#3 (Octave + minor seventh).
Play chromatically down the keyboard, until you reach C1/A#2.
The beats should get slower as you descend down the keyboard.

This check has limited use on small pianos.

## Tuning C1 down to A0

The pattern for tuning this section will be as follows:

    1. Tune the Octave

Example: Tuning B1
    1. Tune B using B2

---

### What are you listening for?

The Octave should be clean.

---

### Checking Bass Octaves

These Bass Octaves can be checked by listening to the beats of the descending **Octave + Augmented Fourth**

Play C1/F#2 (Octave-Augmented Fourth).
Play chromatically down the keyboard, until you reach A0/D#2
The beats should get slower as you descend down the keyboard.

This check has limited use on small pianos.

---

### What do you need to do?

Tune B0 down to A0 using the above instructions.

# Review

The interval tests for this section work very well in pianos that have a nice scale. For the most part, grand pianos that are at least 5'2" will be pretty good. Most studio pianos that are at least 45" tall will not be bad either.

What are some of the tests you would need to drop on some pianos? The first would be the step comparing the minor third to the Major sixth. *(Example E3/G3 equals G3/E4)*. The next one to go will be the Major 3rd/minor3rd test. *(E3/G#3 is slower than E3/G3)*.

On some pianos you will find that the Major 3rd and minor 3rd *(E3/G#3 is slower than E3/G3)* will be equal to each other. Otherwise tune the Octave, and check the Fifth and Fourth above the lower note. At some point you can only use single and double octaves and that's the best you can do.

There are a number of small pianos that use wound strings in the tenor, or even in the temperment area. The nodal influence on a wound string is greater than on a plain steel string. When there is a wound string for the lower tone and a steel string for the upper tone, you will note a slowing of the beating of wide intervals and a speeding up of the narrow intervals, as compared to the beating of adjacent similar intervals which are sounded by pairs of wrapped or plain strings. When this occurs, the thirds and sixths will beat faster. That's ok. It's always better to give preference to the Fourths and Fifths.

One more note. The thirds should get slower as you move down the keyboard. At some point when the beat rate gets too slow, change to the tenth or even seventeenths. These will get slower as you move down the keyboard as well.

As with the temperment, bass octaves can be customized. For instance, by making the thirds and tenths beat a bit faster as you move down the keyboard, you will automatically be tuning a wider octave. There might be an advantage in this, especially when tuning smaller pianos. It will make the piano sound bigger. Again, this is something that you should be thinking about later on. I just want to make you aware that there is room to customize each tuning to make the piano sound as good as it can. Remember, our objective is not simply to follow a set of rules, but to bring out the best sound the piano can produce.

# Tuning
the
# Treble

# Tuning F#4 to F5

The pattern for this section is as follows:

1. Tune the Octave
2. Listen to the Fifth
3. Listen to the Fourth

Example: Tune F#4

1. Tune F#4 using F#3
2. Listen to B3/F#4 (Fifth)
3. Listen to C#4/F#4 (Fourth)

## What are you listening for?

The Octave should be fairly clean sounding.
The Fifth should have a very slow beat.
The Fourth will have a beat, but not objectionable.

After making any corrections, begin with F#3 to F#4 and listen to the octaves chromatically up the piano.

## Checking the Octaves Part I

After tuning the entire section (F#4 to F5)
listen to the Octave-Fifth.
Example: B2 to F#4

Move chromatically up the keyboard listening to all the Octave/Fifths.

These intervals should be fairly quiet.

Adjust any intervals that seem out of place.

## Checking the Octaves Part II

After tuning the entire section (F#4 to F5)
listen to the 10ths.
Example: C#4 to F5

Move chromatically down the keyboard listening to all the 10ths.

These intervals should progressively get slower.

Adjust any intervals that seem out of place.

The 10ths will be a little faster than the 3rds

Example: D3/F#3 is slower than D3/F#4.

## Tuning F#5 to F6

The pattern for this section is as follows:

1. First, tune the notes in this section using the note one octave below.
2. Then, check each note using the Octave-Fifth.
3. Finally, listen to the Seventeenth compared to the tenth (same reference note).

Example: F#5

1. Tune F#5 using F#4.
2. Check the Octave-Fifth B3 to F#5.
3. Compare the Seventeenth to the Tenth D3/F#5 and D3 to F#4.
   *The Seventeenth will beat a little faster than the Tenth.*

---

**What are you listening for?**

The Octaves should be rather clean.
The Octave-Fifth should also be rather clean.
The Seventeenths will beat faster than the Tenths
(The Tenth and Seventeenth have the same reference note).

---

After making any corrections, begin with F#4 to F#5 and listen to the octaves chromatically up and down the scale. Now listen to the double octave beginning with F#3 to F#5 and listen up and down the scale.

### How fast should the seventeenth beat?
Compare the M6 to the 17th.
Example: F3 to A5 (17th).
F3 to D4 should beat the same as F3 to A5.

### Checking the Octaves Part I
After tuning the entire section (F#5 to F6)
listen to the Octave-Fifth.
Example: B4 to F#6
Move chromatically up the keyboard listening to all the Octave/Fifths.
These intervals should be fairly quiet.
Adjust any intervals that seem out of place.

### Checking the Octaves Part II
After tuning the entire section (F#5 to F6)
listen to the Seventeenths.
Example: D3 to F#5
Move chromatically up the keyboard listening to all the Seventeenths.
These intervals should progressively get faster.
Adjust any intervals that seem out of place.

## Tuning F#6 to C7

The pattern for this section is as follows:

1. Tune each note using the octave below as the reference note.
2. Listen to the Octave-Fifth.
3. Listen to the Seventeenth.

Example: Tune F#6

1. Tune F#6 using F#5.
2. Check the Octave-Fifth B4 to F#6.
3. Compare the Seventeenth to the Tenth D4/F#6 and D4 to F#5.
   *The Seventeenth will beat a little faster than the Tenth.*

## What are you listening for?

The Octaves should be clean.
The Octave-Fifth should be clean or almost clean.
The Seventeenths will beat faster than the Tenths (The Tenth and Seventeenth having the same reference note).

## Checking the Octaves Part I

After tuning the entire section (F#6 to C7)
listen to the Octave-Fifth.
Example: B4 to F#6
Move chromatically up the keyboard listening to all the Octave/Fifths.
These intervals should be fairly quiet.
Adjust any intervals that seem out of place.

## Checking the Octaves Part II

After tuning the entire section (F#6 to C7)
listen to the Seventeenths.
Example: D4 to F#6
Move chromatically down the keyboard listening to all the Seventeenths.
These intervals should progressively get faster as you play up the keyboard.
Adjust any intervals that seem out of place.

# Tuning C7 to C8

The pattern for this section is as follows:

1. Tune each note using the octave below as the reference note.
2. Listen to the Octave-Fifth.

Example: Tune C#7.

1. Tune C#7 using C#6.
2. Check the Octave-Fifth F#5 to C#7.

## What are you listening for?

The Octaves should be clean.
The Octave-Fifth should be clean.

## Checking the Octaves Part I

After tuning the entire section (C#7 to C8) listen to the Octave-Fifth.
Example: F#5 to C#7.
Move chromatically up the keyboard listening to all the Octave/Fifths.
These intervals should be fairly quiet.
Adjust any intervals that seem out of place.

## Checking the Octaves Part II

After tuning the entire section (C#7 to C8)

listen to the Double Octaves.

Example: C#5 to C#7.

Move chromatically up the keyboard.

Adjust any intervals that seem out of place.

# Review

The key to this section is the Octave/Fifth and the smooth Tenths and Seventeenths. This approach will allow you to predict and produce precise, uniform results. Your octaves should be clean and bright. This should be particularly true on large pianos. But on smaller pianos, you might want to allow for a more noticeable beat in the Fifth and Octave-Fifth, so that the octave is clean. Learning how to compromise comes with experience. This brings to mind the relationship between the "**Major Third / Major Tenth**" test and the fifth inside this octave interval. The more quiet you make the fifth, the wider the octave and the faster the Major Tenth will be than the Major Third. As I said, this can be an issue on small pianos. The piano will tell you how clean to make the fifth without compromising the octave with a noticeable beat. Knowing your client may help in knowing how wide to make the octave as well. Further, on page 46, there is a box that asks the question; **How fast should the seventeenth beat?** This is an important test. The seventeenth should never beat faster than the sixth. Use this test as high up the scale as you can hear the beats.

Again, as you gain experience, you may find you are able to make some minor variations to bring out the best tone. For instance, you may choose not to stretch the last octave, C7-C8, quite as much as the octaves below it. Make a habit of listening to your work with a critical ear.

# Tuning
the
# Unisons

# Unison Tuning

Tuning good unisons is essential. It is quite possible to tune all the unisons beatless and yet have some of them, or maybe all of them, improperly tuned. How is that possible?

Sometimes when you strike a unison, you hear a beat just begin to develop and then disappear. Or sometimes when you strike a unison you will hear one beat and then it disappears. Why is that?

When a unison is *almost* in perfect tune, the design of the soundboard and bridge will force the strings to vibrate in phase, causing the tone to be beatless. If we were to leave these unisons in this state, we would loose the beauty of our tuning rather quickly. Why?

First, any change of tension due to changes in humidity will be sufficient to disallow the soundboard and bridge assembly to force phase the strings to be beatless. So beats will now appear in the unisons.

Second, when the soundboard and bridge assembly force phase the strings to be beatless, the string vibrations are being either slowed or hurried. This results in the tone having a *rough* quality. It simply will not have the smooth, round tone it should.

How does one learn to tune a proper unison? Practice, practice, practice. Actually, the rough quality of a unison will appear on either side of a dead match in frequency. So, you want to put the unison right in between these two areas of roughness. Listen for the beauty of the tone.

In the real world this is not always possible. Pianos vary in quality and design. You will notice on vertical pianos, in the area where the bridge is notched or cut out to clear a plate strut, the unisons are particularly difficult to tune.

Tuning unisons might be compared to sharpening a chisel. There are several steps in sharpening a chisel? Depending on the condition of the edge, one might begin with the *grinding wheel*, then progress to the:

*Course stone - Medium stone - Fine stone - Very fine stone—Leather strap.*

You can't start with the grinding wheel and then skip to the leather strap. The same approach might be applied to tuning unisons.

After all the center strings have been tuned, the strip felt is removed. Begin in the bass and tune the unisons all the way up the piano. Or, begin in the treble and tune all the unisons down to the bass. Another method would be to begin at the tenor end of the bass section and tune down. Then begin at the lower end of the tenor and tune up to the top of the piano. I prefer the latter method.

On the first pass, tune the unisons beatless, but set a pace that will allow you to move along. In other words, don't spend too much time on any one unison. You're not necessarily looking for that very fine edge yet.

We have stated that it is possible to have a unison beatless but not really in tune. The unison may be somewhat sharp after the first pass, but we want to be able to put that leather edge on it.

Now that you have made the first pass, the entire piano has settled down. On the next pass, we're really trying to hone the unisons. Your ears are more sensitive. Your hands are feeling the tuning pin right through the tuning lever. You'll discover that by nature, you will be working as if with a very fine stone. The edge of the unisons will become very sharp, and not just beatless.

Now comes the time for the leather strap. On this pass you'll really be bringing out the beauty of each unison. Particularly will you notice how the manor in which you strike the unison produces different types of sounds. For example, when you make a loud, medium and soft tone, does the unison sound different? What happens when you listen to long sustained tones compared with rapid short tones. You'll discover that playing the notes in the tenor section with a medium blow and listening to the sustain is very useful. That method is not nearly as effective in the high treble section where a more rapid short blow will produce better results.

There is nothing like a sharp chisel when working with wood, and there is nothing that will bring out the beauty of your tuning like leather sharp unisons.

## Patterns for Tuning Unisons

There are several patterns for tuning unisons. Sometimes the piano is **off pitch** enough that a fine tuning is simply not possible. In such an instance, after tuning all the center strings, remove the strip mute and *re-insert* it so that you mute every other unison. Then begin at the tenor end of the piano and tune one string of each unison until you get to the top. Re-install the strip mute so as to block the string that you just tuned and repeat this process again. After tuning the tenor and treble sections tune the unisons in the bass.

The advantage of this system is twofold. First, the manner in which the tension is increased along the scale is more gradual. Therefore, the piano will be somewhat more stable. Second, this method will allow you to move along at a fairly quick pace, which also contributes to the stability.

The next step would be to strip mute the entire scale again and check all the center strings. No doubt you will find that some things have changed. So, make any necessary adjustments to the piano before tuning the unisons again.

This time when tuning the unisons you will probably choose another pattern. After removing the felt strip mute, begin in the low end of the tenor section and tune up to the top of the piano. Using a rubber mute you would block the left string of the unison and tune the right string to the center string. Then move the mute so as to block the right string of the unison and tune the left string to the center string. Once you've reached the top, go back and tune the bass section. A small variation would be to begin in the bass section and then move to the tenor section and tune the unisons to the top.

When you want to perform your very best tuning, the next pattern would be a good choice. This approach assumes that the piano is very well tuned to begin with. If there is such a thing as a "Concert Tuning", this pattern will allow for the most accurate results.

## Tuning Unisons C8 to C7

The pattern for this section begins with C8 and moves down to C7. At this point the entire scale is still strip muted. You will pull the strip mute out one unison at a time. You will use rubber mutes, especially at the breaks. Follow this procedure:

1. Tune the right string to the center string beatless. *(the strip mute is still muting the left string of C8)*
2. Listen to the center/right string and the octave below
3. Listen to the center/right string and the Octave Fifth below
4. Pull the strip mute out between B7 and C8 only and block right string with a rubber mute. (*sometimes C8 is difficult to block*)
5. Tune the left string to the center string beatless
6. Listen to the center/left string and the octave below
7. Listen to the center/left string and the Octave Fifth below

Example: Tune C8

1. Tune C8 right string to C8 center string.
2. Check the Octave below.
   C7 to C8 center/ right together.
3. Check the Octave Fifth below.
   F6 to C8 center/right together.
4. Pull the strip mute out between B7 and C8 only.
5. With a rubber mute block the right string of C8. (*if possible*)
6. Tune C8 left string to C8 center string.
7. Check the Octave below.
   C7 to C8 center/left together.
8. Check the Octave Fifth below.
   F6 to C8 center/left together.

---

**What are you listening for?**

Unisons should be beatless.
The Octaves should be very clean.
The Octave-Fifth should be fairly quite.

## Tuning the Balance of the Unisons

This pattern continues for the balance of the piano. Tune the right string to the center, remove the strip mute from the left string and then blocking the right string tune the left string to the center. In the bass just remove the strip mute and tune the unisons.

Checking the individual strings of the unison to reference notes used to tune the center string can be very useful in tuning the unison, especially in the high treble area. As you move down the scale, it might be easier to find the sweet spot without interval testing. In the bass and lower tenor area, interval testing is usually not necessary. However, it is a tool you can use to help you make the right decisions.

There is another advantage to tuning the unisons with this pattern. Even before tuning the unison, you can quickly check to see if the middle string has moved. Compare the note with a reference note. Use one of the test intervals for the area in which you are working. After tuning the outside strings to the middle, you can again quickly compare the completed unison with the same reference note.

After tuning all the unisons, go back and check your work. You will probably find that there is room to make a few adjustments here and there. I do this, not just by listening to each unison, but by putting my tuning hammer on the outside string of each unison and feeling if the tuning pin is sitting right in the middle of the sweet spot - between the two rough areas of a beatless unison.

## Helpful Hints

Strike the key about one time per second with a rather soft touch. There are two advantages. The false beats don't have as much time to develop, and the partials you need to focus on, which decay rather quickly in this area, are thus emphasized.

Sometimes it's helpful to tune each string of the unison separately to the original reference note. Then listen to the two strings of the unison again. Make any fine adjustment to leave the unison as clean and pure as possible.

Temporarily block the duplex scales with a very thin felt, such as nameboard felt, to block unwanted noise.

Again, strike the key about one time per second with a rather soft touch. Stability of the unison can be enhanced if you can leave a bit more tension on the string segment right in front of the tuning pin. This can be accomplished in a couple of ways. One would be by making the final movement of the tuning pin in a clockwise direction. This is a movement so small that it doesn't change the frequency of the string, nor would cause the string to go sharp with a hard blow to the key.

# Conclusion

I hope these instructions will help you to accomplish your goals. I would suggest that if you're serious about this profession, you should contact the Piano Technicians Guild. The **P**iano **T**echnicians **G**uild is a not-for-profit association of piano technicians. Based in Kansas City, MO, the PTG has members throughout the USA and Canada as well as some in other countries.

The **PTG** has two major functions:

- To provide education for professional piano technicians and;

- To operate an examinations program to qualify technicians as

**Registered Piano Technician RPT.**

The **PTG's** educational offerings include:

- The monthly *Piano Technicians Journal*, a technical magazine covering many phases of piano work, and other publications of a technical nature.

- Also, conventions and seminars with institutes on technical subjects.

PTG runs a comprehensive examinations program. Since piano tuning is not a licensed profession, PTG has set up voluntary standards of quality workmanship and examinations to test for them. Examinations cover tuning, regulation of actions, and repairs, as well as a basic knowledge of piano design and construction. Only after examinees have passed these tests can they identify themselves as Registered Piano Technician (RPT). With over 3,500 members throughout the world, PTG is an important force in the piano industry.

**Visit the Piano Technicians Guild at:
www.ptg.org**

## Questions or Suggestions?

Please contact me at:
RickButlerRPT@comcast.net

Please visit my website at: www.rickbutler.org

# Appendix

# Grand Piano

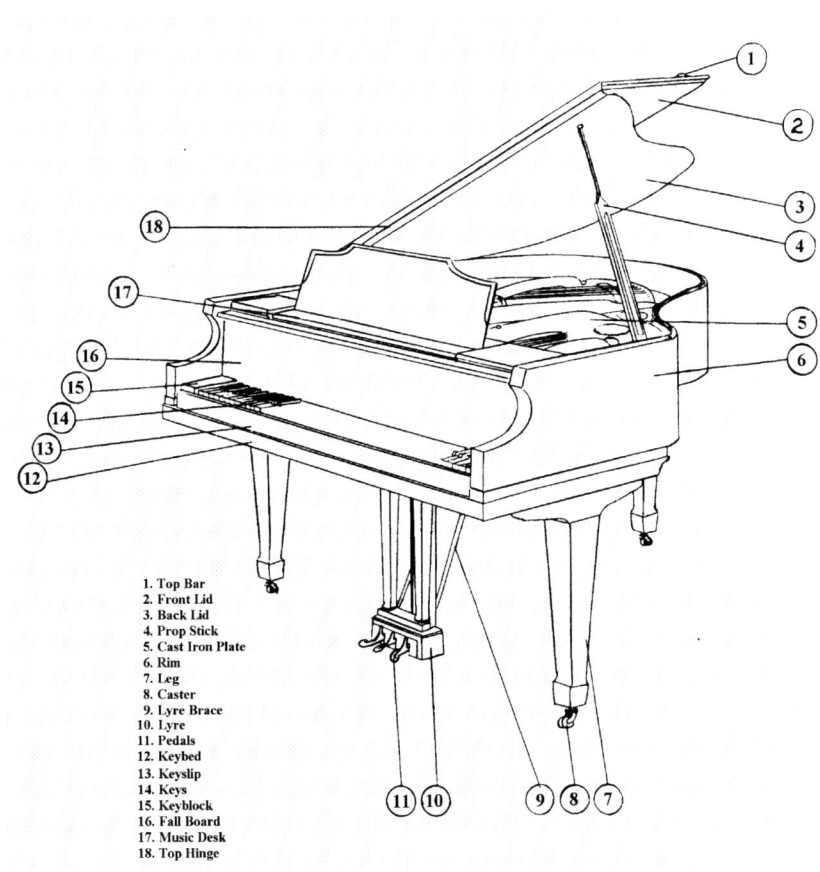

1. Top Bar
2. Front Lid
3. Back Lid
4. Prop Stick
5. Cast Iron Plate
6. Rim
7. Leg
8. Caster
9. Lyre Brace
10. Lyre
11. Pedals
12. Keybed
13. Keyslip
14. Keys
15. Keyblock
16. Fall Board
17. Music Desk
18. Top Hinge

**Case Nomenclature**

# Vertical Piano

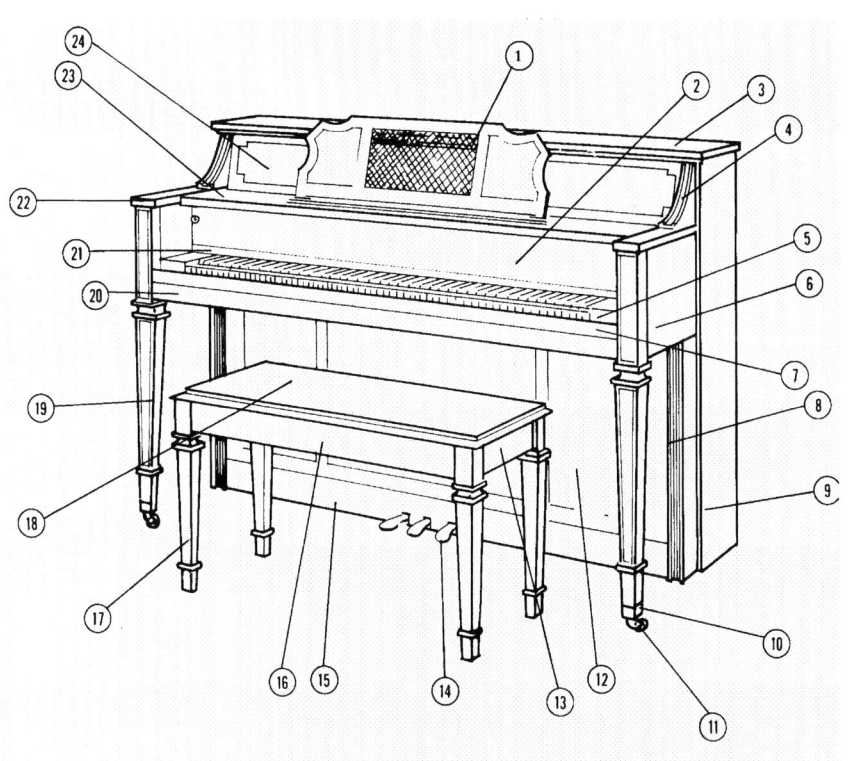

**Case Nomenclature**

1. Music Desk
2. Fallboard
3. Top
4. Armblock
5. Cheek block
6. Arm
7. Key Slip
8. Side Stile
9. Side
10. Ferrule
11. Caster
12. Bottom Panel
13. Bench End Rail
14. Pedal
15. Pedal Rail
16. Bench Side Rail
17. Bench Leg
18. Bench Top
19. Truss Leg
20. Keybed
21. keystop rail
22. Arm Cap
23. Shelf
24. Shelf Back Rail

# Biography

Richard (Rick) Butler, a craftsman member of the Piano Technicians Guild (PTG), has been a full time – and full service – piano technician for more than 30 years. His piano rebuilding experience encompasses work on all components of the instrument, including re-stringing, bridge and soundboard repair/replacement, pin block replacement, keyframe and key manufacture, as well as complete action, underlever, and trap work repair, replacement, and regulation. In addition to running his own shop, Rick has served as chief technician for two large universities and as shop foreman for a major piano dealer. His service as concert technician includes many years with the National Symphony Orchestra, the Kennedy Center, and the White House. Within his PTG Chapter (Washington D.C.), he has served his profession in various capacities. He has also lectured at local, regional and national meetings. The videos and texts in his current technical series are designed to detail principles and practices of successful piano maintenance.